FOUNDATIONS II

Basic Blocks for Building a Life of Faith

John Cervone & Arnold Fleagle

✝✝ Christian Publications

CAMP HILL, PENNSYLVANIA

Walking with the Word
Bible Studies

Christian Publications, Inc.
3825 Hartzdale Drive, Camp Hill, PA 17011
www.cpi-horizon.com

Faithful, biblical publishing since 1883

ISBN: 0-87509-780-4

CONTENTS

Introduction

The most significant decision anyone can ever make is to decide to follow Jesus Christ as Savior and Lord. *Foundations II* is a course of study that has been designed to build up your faith—to help you gain a firm foundation and grow in spiritual maturity.

Jesus tells us that our faith—what we believe and how we live—is like the wise man who builds his house upon the rock. When the winds of trouble come and beat against the house, it will stand (see Matthew 7:24–27).

Foundations II is designed to be used in Sunday school classes, small groups or individual study. It contains six lessons. You may choose to do one lesson a week or spend two weeks on each lesson.

The *Leader's Guide,* which begins on page 53, provides answers to most questions and additional background material to assist you in your study.

Our prayer for you is that your faith will grow as you follow Jesus Christ and permit Him to be Lord of every facet of your life.

We readily recognize David Fessenden of Christian Publications who assisted us in creating the proper format to present this series of studies. Also, we are grateful for the many hours of labor that were invested by Gail Roso, our church secretary at Stow Alliance Fellowship.

By His grace,
John C. Cervone and Arnold R. Fleagle

STUDY ONE

The Lordship of
Jesus Christ

The story is told of the cathedral in Freiburg, Germany, which contained a famous organ. One day a man entered and asked to play it. The custodian resisted the request, but he eventually granted permission.

The guest sat down and began to play music which moved the sexton to take a seat and eventually the man began to weep over the beautiful sounds that emerged from the instrument he was entrusted to care and guard.

When the stranger stood up and began to leave, the custodian inquired, "Who are you?"

The visitor replied, "I am Mendelssohn."

The old man threw up his hands and cried, "And to think I almost refused to let you play my organ."

When Jesus Christ enters our lives, He turns disharmony to harmony and noise to music. He tunes us, removing the sins which cause discordant and displeasing sounds. However, He does not want to just tune our instrument—He wants to play it.

It is very detrimental to our Christian lives if we view Jesus Christ as only the piano tuner and not the piano player. He is not only Savior, He is Lord.

Too many unbelievers come to the Master for a tuning, rather than allowing Him to take control of their lives. This is a tragedy, for the Master can bring forth music that will be far superior to our own feeble attempts to produce the sounds of the redeemed.

We are the custodians of our lives. We grant permission or deny it. We issue clearance or withhold it. It is crucial that the Christian realize that a decision to accept Jesus Christ is only the initial step in God's plan. He wants to write a symphony through the gifts and talents and circumstances of our lives.

A custodian is usually a poor organ player! It is time to take inventory of who is in control of your life and all the resources it represents. Jesus is your Savior but He is also your Lord.

Walking into the Scriptures

Read Romans 10:9-13

This passage tells a person how to be saved. Notice how many times the term "Lord" is used in this salvation context.

1. What is the confession in Romans 10:9?

2. According to Romans 10:12, Jesus Christ is Lord of which peoples?

3. Everyone is to call on whom to be saved?

Read Acts 2:36

1. What did the people do to Jesus Christ?

2. What did God make Jesus?

Read First Corinthians 6:18-20

1. What are the Corinthian believers told to flee from?

2. What analogy is used regarding the body of the Christian?

3. Why does a Christian no longer have ownership of his or her body?

4. The body is to be used for what purpose?

Read First Corinthians 12:1-3

1. No one speaking by the Spirit of God says what about Jesus?

2. Those who say, "Jesus is Lord," do so under whose influence?

Walking It into My Life

Discipleship is not an easy road. Remember the broad and easy road leads to destruction (Matthew 7:13). If Jesus is to be Lord of our lives, then He has given us a challenge which contains three elements:

Read Luke 9:23

1. Challenge one: What does it mean to "deny one-self?" Compare your response to that of Jesus in Luke 14:33.

2. Challenge two: What does it mean to "take up your cross?" (Hint: Think of what Jesus did when He literally took up His cross.) How often is this to be done?

3. Challenge three: If we "follow Him," who does the leading? Who is doing the leading in your life today? What practical steps can you take to ensure that you are following Jesus as the Lord of your life?

Read Mark 12:30

If Jesus is to be Lord, then He needs to be obeyed. Jesus was asked by the teachers of the law, "Of all the commandments, which is the most important?" In Mark 12:30 we find His response.

1. Whom are we to love?

2. With what are we to love?

3. What part of the person is left out of loving the Lord?

4. List any parts of your life that do not demonstrate your love of the Lord. Prayerfully ask the Lord to grant you His power to bring these under His control.

Walking a Little Deeper

Read Acts 2:36

In this verse the apostle Peter did not proclaim Jesus only as Savior, but as both Lord and Christ. Using a Bible dictionary (your Bible may have one in the back), look up definitions for Jesus, Lord and Christ. What do these tell about Jesus?

Read Philippians 2:6-11

1. What two actions, mentioned in verses 10 and 11, recognize the Lordship of Christ?

2. Memorize Philippians 2:10-11. Check here when memorized. ☐

STUDY TWO

The Holy Spirit

You may be familiar with hymns or choruses which speak of the Trinity, or "God in Three Persons"—Father, Son and Holy Spirit. How can God be one and three at the same time? It can be compared to heating a container of water. If heated quickly and if the heat levels are varied, the water in a single moment of time can be solid, liquid and gas. One substance, in one second of time, can exist in three expressions.

The Holy Spirit is a Person. He is invisible, but like the wind which you cannot see, you are able to see the results. The Spirit lives inside the believer, yet He also operates externally to the believer. He is not limited by time or space. He is all-knowing, all-powerful and ever-present.

The Holy Spirit is the Christian's invisible partner. Can you remember your first day of school? What would it have meant to you to have an "invisible partner" who would exercise protection, give insight to the learning process, provide words for you to speak, enable you to ask good questions, comfort you when you were threatened and serve as a guide through all the day's activities? These roles and more are fulfilled by the Holy Spirit in the life and work of the believer.

Jesus has ascended into heaven to sit at the Father's right hand, but the Father has sent another to enable, empower and equip the believer to do the work of ministry and to live a dynamic Christian life.

Walking into the Scriptures

Read John 14:16-18

1. What did Jesus ask of the Father?

2. What names are given to the Holy Spirit in this passage?

3. Where is the Holy Spirit in relationship to the believer?

Read John 16:13-14

1. What major role does the Spirit perform regarding the believer?

2. What major role does the Spirit perform regarding Jesus?

Read Romans 8:26-27

1. Why must the Spirit help us?

2. What discipline of the Christian life is mentioned in this passage?

3. How does the Spirit assist us in this discipline?

Read Ephesians 5:18-20

1. What does Paul prohibit in this passage?

2. What does Paul command in this passage?

3. What activities do you think are mentioned in this passage which could be traced to the fullness of the Holy Spirit?

Walking It into My Life

Read Ephesians 4:30 and Acts 5:3

The Holy Spirit is the third person of the Trinity: God the Father, God the Son and God the Holy Spirit. Although we find little difficulty comprehending that the Holy Spirit is God, it is often harder to understand that He is a person, not some impersonal force or mere influence.

1. What two types of offenses toward the Holy Spirit are mentioned in Ephesians 4:30 and Acts 5:3?

2. Can you imagine an impersonal object or force that could be offended in this way? What can we then conclude about the Holy Spirit?

3. Look also at Acts 5:4. From this verse what can we conclude about the Holy Spirit?

4. In Scripture symbols are often used to characterize a person. This is particularly true for the Holy Spirit. Identify the symbol representing the Holy Spirit in each of the following verses:

    a. Matthew 3:11—
    b. Matthew 3:16—
    c. John 3:6-8—
    d. John 7:37-39—

5. Can you think of implied meanings for some of these symbols of the Holy Spirit?

Walking a Little Deeper

The Holy Spirit works in the lives of believers in many ways, having many roles identified in Scripture. Read each Scripture passage below and describe the role of the Holy Spirit.

Matthew 10:10 _____

John 3:5 _____

John 14:26 _____

John 16:13-15 _____

John 16:8-11 _____

John 14:16 _____

Romans 8:26-28 _____

1 Corinthians 12:4-11_____

The Holy Spirit fills these and many other roles in the believer's life. As you read the Bible, keep your eyes open for other ministries of the Holy Spirit.

After completing this assignment, reflect upon God the Holy Spirit who indwells you as a disciple of Christ. Take a moment in prayer to thank God for the Holy Spirit in your life.

STUDY THREE

The Will of God

What is the will of God for my life? Where does He want me to go? What does He want me to do? Whom does He want me to marry? Where does He want me to go to school? Is there a specific city or town I should live in? God's will for the Christian's life encompasses every sector of his or her experience!

How does one discover God's will? As Charles Swindoll points out in the following story, some believers use methods that are less than effective:

One collegian was looking for a car. As a Christian he pledged to discover God's will for his purchase of a vehicle. One night he had a series of dreams. Everything in those dreams was *yellow*. The next day he walked through several car lots and finally found a car that was *yellow* inside and out. He didn't bother to have it road tested or to ask a reputable mechanic to check it out. It was yellow, so he bought it. As you might expect, *it turned out to be a lemon.*[1]

The Word of God is very specific on certain aspects of God's will. The Ten Commandments provide some clear guidelines for whom we worship, how we speak, whom we honor and how we treat other people. However, there are many "street corners" we arrive at which provide no clear and explicit commandments.

Gary Friesen, in his strategic book, *Decision Making and the Will of God*, provides a checklist for believers to consult when making choices. If the Bible does not specifically command or prohibit an action, Friesen suggests that the child of God access other road signs, including: (1) inner witness, or what you sense God is telling you to do; (2) personal desires; (3) circumstances; (4) mature counsel; and (5) common sense.[2]

The will of God is nonnegotiable for the believer. Every major decision should be weighed with God's Word in mind, and where there is doubt, prayer and consultation with mature Christians should be sought out and evaluated. The Holy Spirit, who lives in each believer, often supplies or withholds His peace to help us determine His will.

Sometimes a number of options may all represent and satisfy God's will. For example, if you are asked to choose between apple, peach or cherry pie for dessert, which pie represents God's choice? None of the choices would be prohibitive; they would all be acceptable—unless, of course, you are watching your weight!

Walking into the Scriptures

Read Matthew 12:46-50

1. What question did Jesus ask in this passage?

2. To whom did Jesus point in answering His own question?

3. What did Jesus say is the deciding factor in being one of His "relatives"?

Read Mark 14:32-36

1. What was Jesus' mood at this moment in His life?

2. What did Jesus ask of His Father regarding the task which was ahead of Him?

3. What was Jesus' final word on the matter?

Read Proverbs 3:5-6

1. In whom should we trust and to what extent should we trust?

2. What should we not lean on?

3. What is the result of acknowledging the Lord?

Read Proverbs 15:22

1. Why do plans fail?

2. What factor for success is suggested in this passage?

3. Who might be included in your network of counselors?

Walking It into My Life

Read Exodus 20:1-17

As mentioned in the introduction to this study topic, the Ten Commandments provide one series of guidelines for understanding God's will for our lives.

1. Using the Ten Commandments, make a list of ten actions that would be outside the will of God.

2. Now make a list of three behaviors outside the will of God that commonly occur in today's society. How do these differ from your list from question 1? How are they similar?

3. Read First Peter 4:1-6 and First John 2:17. Identify one area where you are or may be headed outside God's will for your life. Pray to God for the power to have victory in this area.

Read Ephesians 6:5-8

You may not personally identify with being a slave, but if, as an employee or student, you are under someone else's authority, you are in the role referred to in this passage as "slaves." These verses tell us how to operate at work or school to be in the will of God.

1. To be in the will of God, what is to be the Christian's standard of performance at work or school?

2. What should not be our primary motivation to do well at work or school? What should be our incentive to do well?

Walking a Little Deeper

Read Proverbs 15:22

1. List the significant decisions you are facing over the next several months. Search the Word of God and pray about them. Gather the appropriate information that may be needed. In addition, seek the counsel of two or three mature Christians. When you have completed these steps check here. ☐

If you are doing this study with a group, be prepared to discuss what you thought of while following these steps. Do you believe you will be in the will of God?

2. This discussion of the will of God may bring to mind your will—the legal document that tells what you want done with what you have left behind after you die. Most people seek the counsel of an attorney in doing this. Consider writing your "will" for what you want done with the life you still have—the will of God for your life. Remember as a Christian you have an "attorney" (advocate) with the Father (1 John 2:1, KJV) and a counselor (John 14:26; see also Study Two) to guide and intercede on your behalf (Romans 8:26-27).

Endnotes

[1] Charles Swindoll, God's Will (Grand Rapids, MI: Zondervan, 1995), 4.

[2] Gary Friesen, Decision Making and the Will of God (Sisters, OR: Multnomah, 1980), 49-57.

STUDY FOUR

Suffering and Healing

In the summer of 1996, the Fleagle family planned a trip to Myrtle Beach, South Carolina, anticipating a relaxing coastal vacation. Unfortunately, we had to schedule the trip around Hurricane Bertha. The storm was tracking up the Atlantic coast and Myrtle Beach was forecast to be the primary site for landfall. When we arrived on the Tuesday following Bertha's arrival, we discovered that the storm which produced so much fear had left incredible waves in its wake. This made for monumental memories for our two sons, Matthew and Marc, as they rejoiced in being whipped about by the above-average breakers.

This experience is an illustration of a marvelous truth: If we can weather the storm, it provides an opportunity to ride the waves that follow it!

Believers must have a correct view of suffering if they are to maximize their Christian life and ministry. We live in an imperfect world. Our bodies are earthen vessels—jars of clay, which sometimes crack and, like Humpty-Dumpty, can't always be mended. We are threatened by the storms of inflation, disease, weather, misunderstanding and competition. When you became a Christian, that did not exempt you from leaky roofs or hospital beds. The difference is in your attitude toward suffering and the benefits you derive from it. The Christian, when given a lemon, asks the Lord for help to make lemonade.

The child of God also understands that God is able to heal. The Word of God, history and contemporary testimonies attest to a God who can and does heal! "I am the LORD, who heals you" is not only a passage from Exodus 15:26, but it can be a reality. Does God *always* heal? No. Does He still heal? Yes! You and I must trust in His character, for His decisions are perfect.

Walking into the Scriptures

Read Romans 5:1-5

1. In Romans 5:1, how does Paul describe the people he is speaking about?

2. What are the two things we are to rejoice in?

3. What does suffering produce?

4. What has God poured into our hearts?

Read First Peter 2:19-24

1. What kind of suffering is commendable before God?

2. Who suffered for you?

3. Where are you to walk?

4. What is the remedy for unjust treatment?

Read Second Corinthians 12:7-10

Paul had been used as God's instrument in healing others, but this passage reveals that his prayer for himself to be healed was not answered with healing. Many believe his "thorn in the flesh" refers to his poor eyesight.

1. How many times did Paul pray for his "thorn in the flesh" to be taken away?

2. What did the Lord tell Paul was the alternative to his healing?

3. Rather than boasting about his strengths and gifts, what did Paul tell the Corinthians he boasted about?

4. When was Paul strong?

Read James 5:14-18

1. Whom should the sick person call?

2. How should the elders anoint the sick person and in whose name?

3. According to James 5:16, what two actions are we to take toward each other?

4. What is James' description of Elijah?

5. What was Elijah able to accomplish?

Walking It into My Life

---

1. Read the scriptural account of the life of Job in chapters 1, 2 and 42 of the book of Job. What adversities did Job encounter (Job 1-2)? How did Job respond and not respond (see 1:21 and 2:10)? Did Job lose all hope in his sufferings (see 13:15)? How did the story of Job's life end (chapter 42)?

2. List some reasons for suffering based on Scripture.

   a. John 9:1-3:

   b. Romans 8:28-29:

   c. 2 Corinthians 1:3-4:

   d. Philippians 1:29:

   e. Hebrews 12:5-11:

If you are doing this study in a group, be prepared to discuss how the Lord has used one of the above reasons for suffering in your life.

Walking a Little Deeper

1. Based on the following Scriptures, let's develop a brief statement concerning divine healing.

   a. Exodus 15:26:

   b. James 5:13-16:

   c. James 1:6:

   d. Philippians 4:6-7:

   e. 1 Thessalonians 5:17:

   f. 2 Corinthians 12:7-9:

Before the next meeting (if you are doing this study in a group), find someone you know who is suffering through an illness. Visit the ill person (perhaps in the company of a mature Christian), share what you have learned and pray for that person's healing. Encourage that person to seek the elders of the church for anointing and prayer.

2. Have you ever personally experienced the Lord's divine healing in your life? If not, are you aware of someone else who has? (If you are doing this study in a group, be prepared to share one or two experiences with the rest of the class concerning these healing events.) Does divine healing mean that a person will not get sick again or die?

STUDY FIVE

Missions

John 3:16 begins with the words, "For God so loved the world . . ."

The heavenly Father embraced the people of this planet with His love and responded to their lostness by sending the world's greatest Person, Jesus Christ, to provide the most incredible gift ever given: eternal life. It was God's intent not to limit salvation to one nation or people or tribe, but to spread the good news to the whole world.

Jesus, as He prepared to say goodbye to His disciples, left them with a command we call the Great Commission. It is recorded in Matthew 28:19-20 and instructs His followers to disperse themselves to all nations.

As Christians we possess the love of God—and that includes a global vision. As Christians we pledge to obey Jesus Christ—and that includes fulfilling the Great Commission.

The child of God is concerned about others who are still lost in their sins and who have never heard or been confronted with ample opportunity to have their lives redeemed and redirected through an encounter with the Savior.

In Cambodia when the grain is ripe, the people live at the fields until the harvest is complete. Everyone participates! Mothers and fathers, sisters and brothers, aunts and uncles, grandmothers and grandfathers—no one is exempt from the harvest. The same should be true of those who claim to be disciples of Jesus Christ. Everyone is called to bring in the harvest of souls; no one is excluded.

In *Missionary Messages*, A.B. Simpson tells of a missionary in Africa who witnessed for one day in a river village. The people were bitterly disappointed that he could not stay longer. Two days later as he approached the village, he observed people watching from the bank. They became wild in their gestures and loud in their cries as they tried to convince him to come ashore. As he continued down the river, he could hear their bitter cries, a lamentation of lost people who were seeking after God.[1]

Aren't you grateful that you heard the saving message? Will others hear because of you—because you pray, because you give, because you go?

Walking into the Scriptures

Read Matthew 28:19-20

1. What does Jesus say His disciples are to do in all nations?

2. Baptism is to be done in whose name?

3. What are we to teach those who respond to the message?

4. What promise does Jesus give, which will extend to the end of the age?

Read Revelation 7:9-11

1. How many were in the great multitude?

2. Who made up the great multitude?

3. What was the cry of the great multitude?

Read Matthew 9:35-38

1. When Jesus saw the crowds, what "word picture" did He compare them to?

2. What was plentiful?

3. What was in short supply?

4. What are we to ask the Lord of the harvest to do?

Walking It into My Life

Read Matthew 24:14

Many today see in this verse of Scripture a motivation for missions. It is sometimes referred to as "bringing back the King." What do you think this phrase means?

Read Acts 1:8

1. What is the necessary prerequisite for successful witnessing and missions?

2. Notice the geography of witnessing, as stated in this verse: first Jerusalem (locally), then Judea (the surrounding region), then Samaria (the region to the north) and finally to the very ends of the earth. What part of the world is not included?

3. List your Jerusalem, Judea, Samaria, etc. Suggest how you might impact each of these areas for the Lord.

Walking a Little Deeper

Read Romans 10:12-17

1. For whom is the gospel message intended? Is anyone not to have the opportunity to hear the good news? With whom do you need to share the good news where God has placed you? Pray for the opportunity to be a good witness for Christ.

2. List the words of action (verbs) in verses 14 and 15. What is the sequence of events leading to salvation? Who does the preaching of the good news? (Note that the Greek word for "sent" in verse 15 is apostello, which literally means "to send out on a mission," from which we get the words apostle and missionary.)

3. Based on verse 16, will everyone who hears the good news accept it? What does this say concerning successful missions?

4. To get a better understanding of what missions is all about, go to your church library and read the biography of a missionary. Check here when finished. ☐

If you are doing this study in a group, be prepared to briefly discuss the missionary's life and mission.

5. There are at least three ways to support missions: You can pray, give and go. Identify a specific mission field and missionary to pray for over the next year. Consider what the Lord would have you joyfully give, from the resources He has given you, to the work of missions. Then do it! Prayerfully consider what your mission field is and whether God is calling you to another field of ministry.

Endnote

1 A.B. Simpson, Missionary Messages (Camp Hill, PA: Christian Publications, Inc., 1987), 64.

STUDY SIX

The Second Coming

Most of us who have moved to a new state or section of the country have heard many of our friends say, "I'm coming to see you." In reality, many of those "predictions" never come true. However, there are friends who are genuine in their intent to comply with their words. When I moved from Mechanicsburg, Pennsylvania to my next church in Stow, Ohio, one of my close friends told me that he would be out to see me. I didn't realize how soon his words would be fulfilled. A business appointment took him near our new home on the very week of our move. As I sat in my new office at the church, I saw two people walking by my window. I took a second look, but I could hardly convince myself that Drew and Barb Park, of central PA, were standing outside my office window. My friend said he would come to see me, and he did—much sooner than I expected. His prediction, his promise, anchored itself in history.

Jesus Christ has integrity. There is no record that any promise, any prediction that He issued during

His three and one-half years of ministry did not come true. He even predicted His own cruel death, and Calvary's wooden cross brought His dark forecast to reality. When our Lord ascended to heaven, He made a promise that He would come again; He would return in a glorious second coming.

This return visit to planet Earth is mentioned over 300 times in the New Testament. The Christian is commanded to prepare for this event, for it could happen at any moment, at the next tick of the clock. The One who promised to return will fulfill His prediction, for He, above any other person, has crystal clear vision and impeccable integrity. He has forewarned us. He has briefed us. He has provided us with ample opportunity. No one exactly knows the time of His return, but believers should heed His warning: "So you also must be ready, because the Son of Man will come at an hour when you do not expect him" (Matthew 24:44).

Walking into the Scriptures

Read Matthew 24:42-44

1. What are we to do until the day of Jesus' return?

2. What is unknown even to the believer?

3. To what does Jesus compare His second coming?

Read Matthew 25:1-13

This is a parable Jesus told to explain the uncertainty of the time of His coming.

1. What is the kingdom of heaven compared to?

2. How are these virgins described in verse 2?

3. What happened because of the bridegroom's delay?

4. Who made it into the banquet?

Read Acts 1:7-11

1. What did Jesus say regarding times and dates?

2. What happened to Jesus in verse 9?

3. Where were the disciples looking?

4. What did the two men dressed in white tell them?

Read Revelation 22:12-14

1. When did Jesus say He was coming?

2. What will Jesus bring with Him?

3. What are His titles in verse 13?

4. What two privileges are extended to those whose robes are washed?

Walking It into My Life

Read Titus 2:11-14

The apostle Paul referred to the second coming of the Lord Jesus Christ as the "blessed hope." The Christian hope is not just something we wish for; it is a strong desire which we are confident will be satisfied. It has been said, "Hope is faith standing on tiptoe!" Throughout the centuries Christians have held true to their faith in the face of persecution and suffering, being consoled in the hope that Jesus Christ is coming again.

1. Based on Paul's teaching from his letter to Titus, as Christians waiting for the "blessed hope," what things should we not be doing?

2. What should Christians be doing?

3. Identify (if you are in a group study, be prepared to discuss) at least one way this teaching on the second coming should impact your daily life.

Read First Thessalonians 4:13-5:11

This passage of Scripture details what is commonly referred to as the rapture of the Church and the subsequent period of tribulation (see also 2 Thessalonians 2:1-12). The rapture is the first phase of Jesus' second coming.

1. Look up in a dictionary the term "rapture" and write a definition.

2. What are the heavenly signs the rapture is occurring, and what is the location of Jesus at the rapture?

3. What is the sequence of events at the rapture?

THE SECOND COMING 51

4. In what ways is the truth of this text an encouragement to you? (If you are in a group study, be prepared to discuss this question.)

Walking a Little Deeper

Read Revelation 20:1-6

The second phase of the second coming of Jesus Christ deals with His physical return to earth. This is often referred to as the millennial kingdom—millennial, because it will last for 1,000 years, a millennium; kingdom, because Jesus Christ, the King of kings, will reign on the earth.

1. What terms are used to refer to the devil?

2. Whom does the beast represent? (See Revelation 13:2b, 4.)

3. Who will experience the first resurrection? Who will not?

4. Who will experience the second death? Who will not?

5. Who will reign with Christ with authority for the thousand years?

In Luke 21:36, Jesus exhorts us to be on the watch and to pray for ourselves concerning the soon coming end-time events. Write down your thoughts on why He might have chosen to emphasize watching and praying.

Christian Growth Inventory

Congratulations! You have completed the *Foundations II* Bible study and you are well on your way in the Christian journey. As you continue in your growth in the Lord, consider these steps that others have found helpful in walking God's way:

____ 1. Write your testimony in one or two paragraphs.

____ 2. Tell someone that you have a personal relationship with Jesus Christ, using your testimony.

____ 3. Find a local church and worship weekly.

____ 4. Develop a daily time of prayer and Bible study.

____ 5. Participate in a small group, such as a Bible study or Sunday school class.

____ 6. Be baptized.

____ 7. Be involved in a ministry in the local church.

____ 8. Join a membership class for your church.

____ 9. Tithe (give ten percent of your income).

____ 10. Observe the Lord's Supper (Communion).

____ 11. Become acquainted with the work of a missionary and pray for his or her ministry.

____ 12. Subscribe to a Christian periodical and read it regularly.

**Walking with the Word
Bible Studies**

Leader's Guide

F*oundations II* is a discipleship course for believers. It is designed to develop in the follower of Jesus Christ an understanding and application of core values which are essential for dynamic Christian living.

The study guide in the beginning of this book asks students to look up specific Scriptures (in the "Walking into the Scriptures" section) and to fill in answers to the questions based on those verses. It also includes sections called "Walking It into My Life" to help students apply what they have studied to their daily lives. The "Walking a Little Deeper" section is for those students who want to tackle a little more challenging material.

Foundations II is designed so that it can be used in Sunday school classes, small groups or for individual study. It contains six lessons. You may choose to do one lesson a week or spend two weeks on each lesson.

This Leader's Guide provides answers and additional background material (in italics) for most of the questions in the study guide. If you are going through this study on your own, the Leader's Guide can be used if you are stuck on a question or would like more information on the things you are learning.

If you are leading a group study, the Leader's Guide includes suggestions (also in italics) to help you keep the discussion on track. It is intended to help you guide the group; it should not be seen as an "answer key" that limits group discussion. Keep in mind that the new believers in your group are looking to you as an example. Determine to be approachable, open and honest. In so doing, they will be more likely to share areas where they are struggling.

As you lead the group, remember Jesus' words in Matthew 28:19–20: "Therefore go and make disciples of all nations, baptizing them in the name of the Father and of the Son and of the Holy Spirit, and teaching them to obey everything I have commanded you. And surely I am with you always, to the very end of the age."

Foundations II is one more disciple-making tool, which, if studied and applied, will facilitate teaching which leads to obedience.

STUDY ONE
The Lordship of Jesus Christ

Walking into the Scriptures

Read Romans 10:9-13

1. What is the confession in Romans 10:9?
   "Jesus is Lord"

2. According to Romans 10:12, Jesus Christ is Lord of which peoples?
   All people

3. Everyone is to call on whom to be saved?
   The name of the Lord

Read Acts 2:36

1. What did the people do to Jesus Christ?
   Crucified Him

2. What did God make Jesus?
   Both Lord and Christ

Read First Corinthians 6:18-20

1. What are the Corinthian believers told to flee from?
Sexual immorality

2. What analogy is used regarding the body of the Christian?
It is the temple of the Holy Spirit.

3. Why does a Christian no longer have ownership of his or her body?
He/She has been purchased.

4. The body is to be used for what purpose?
To honor God

Read First Corinthians 12:1-3

1. No one speaking by the Spirit of God says what about Jesus?
Jesus is cursed.

2. Those who say, "Jesus is Lord," do so under whose influence?
The Holy Spirit

Walking It into My Life

Read Luke 9:23

1. Challenge one: What does it mean to "deny oneself?" Compare your response to that of Jesus in Luke 14:33.
Denying oneself means to willingly sacrifice that which you may hold most dear. Literally, it means to give up control over your life—to "give up all you have." In Luke 14:26, Jesus compared this to "hating" father, mother, spouse, children, brothers and sisters . . . even one's own life! Here "hating" means to disregard the demands of others or even of ourselves when faced with the demand of allegiance to the Lord.

2. Challenge two: What does it mean to "take up your cross?" How often is this to be done?

Taking up your cross means accepting the death of your "right" to live as you choose. You choose now to live your life for the Lord Jesus Christ. As Savior and Lord, He has bought you with His blood and is Lord of your life. Compare Luke 9:23 to Galatians 2:20. It has been said that the Christian spiritually needs to "attend his own funeral" every day.

3. Challenge three: If we "follow Him," who does the leading? Who is doing the leading in your life today? What practical steps can you take to ensure that you are following Jesus as the Lord of your life?

Jesus Christ, who is the Lord, does the leading. Most of us still take the lead in our lives, but the more we get to know Christ and what He expects of us, the easier it is to follow Him. Daily Bible study and fellowship with the Lord in prayer will equip us to yield the lordship of our lives to Christ.

Read Mark 12:30

If Jesus is to be Lord, then He needs to be obeyed. Jesus was asked by the teachers of the law, "Of all the commandments, which is the most important?" In Mark 12:30 we find His response.

1. Whom are we to love?
   The Lord our God

2. With what are we to love?
   All our heart, soul, mind and strength

You may want to note and discuss:

a. The heart is the center of one's thoughts and feelings, the essence of a person's life.

b. The soul comes from a form of the Greek word for "breath," which has to do with the living of life.

c. Mind literally means the deep thoughts of life, the understanding of life.

d. Strength refers to the ability or power that is exerted; the might of life.

3. What part of the person is left out of loving the Lord?
Nothing. Jesus is Lord of all.

4. List any parts of your life that do not demonstrate your love of the Lord. Prayerfully ask the Lord to grant you His power to bring these under His control.
Discuss some potential areas like finances, thought-life and priorities.

Walking a Little Deeper

Read Acts 2:36

In this verse the apostle Peter did not proclaim Jesus only as Savior, but as both Lord and Christ. Using a Bible dictionary (your Bible may have one in the back), look up definitions for Jesus, Lord and Christ. What do these tell about Jesus?

Jesus = Savior
Christ = Anointed One
Lord = Sovereign

Jesus is the Anointed One sent from God, the Father, who saves us and is sovereign over all things.

Read Philippians 2:6-11

1. What two actions, mentioned in verses 10 and 11, recognize the Lordship of Christ?
Verse 10: Knees bow, a form of nonverbal communication; body language
Verse 11: Tongues confess, verbal communication acknowledging Jesus is Lord

2. Memorize Philippians 2:10-11.

Encourage the members of your group to be diligent in "hiding the Word in their hearts." Reciting the verse before the group for the purpose of accountability should be voluntary, however.

STUDY TWO
The Holy Spirit

Walking into the Scriptures

Read John 14:16-18

1. What did Jesus ask of the Father?
To give another Counselor

2. What names are given to the Holy Spirit in this passage?
Counselor, The Spirit of truth

3. Where is the Holy Spirit in relationship to the believer?
He lives within.

Read John 16:13-14

1. What major role does the Spirit perform regarding the believer?
Guides the believer into all truth

2. What major role does the Spirit perform regarding Jesus?
He brings glory to Jesus.

Read Romans 8:26-27

1. Why must the Spirit help us?
We are weak.

2. What discipline of the Christian life is mentioned in this passage?
Prayer

3. How does the Spirit assist us in this discipline?
He intercedes for us.

Read Ephesians 5:18-20

1. What does Paul prohibit in this passage?
Getting drunk on wine

2. What does Paul command in this passage?
Be filled with the Holy Spirit.

3. What activities do you think are mentioned in this passage which could be traced to the fullness of the Holy Spirit?
a. *Speaking to one another with psalms, hymns and spiritual songs*
b. *Singing and making music in your heart*
c. *Always giving thanks*

Walking It into My Life

Read Ephesians 4:30 and Acts 5:3

1. What two types of offenses toward the Holy Spirit are mentioned in Ephesians 4:30 and Acts 5:3?
Grieving Him and lying to Him

2. Can you imagine an impersonal object or force that could be offended in this way? What can we then conclude about the Holy Spirit?
No; being grieved or lied to requires personality. We must conclude, based on the truth of Scripture, that the Holy Spirit is a Person.

3. Look also at Acts 5:4. From this verse what can we conclude about the Holy Spirit?

The Holy Spirit is God, too!

4. In Scripture symbols are often used to characterize a person. This is particularly true for the Holy Spirit. Identify the symbol representing the Holy Spirit in each of the following verses:

a. Matthew 3:11—Fire
b. Matthew 3:16—The dove
c. John 3:6-8—Wind
d. John 7:37-39—Water

5. Can you think of implied meanings for some of these symbols of the Holy Spirit?

Fire—The presence and power of God (Exodus 3:2-6 and Hebrews 12:29)

The dove—Love (Song of Songs 5:2), purity (Song of Songs 6:9), peace (Genesis 8:8-12), innocence (Matthew 10:16) and beauty (Song of Songs 1:15)

Wind—Life and power (John 3:8)

Water—Refreshment and satisfaction (John 4:14)

Walking a Little Deeper

The Holy Spirit works in the lives of believers in many ways, having many roles identified in Scripture. Read each Scripture passage below and define the role of the Holy Spirit.

Matthew 10:10	*Speech writer*
John 3:5	*Doctor*
John 14:26	*Teacher*
John 16:13-15	*Reporter*
John 16:8-11	*Policeman*
John 14:16	*Defense attorney*
Romans 8:26-28	*Operator*
1 Corinthians 12:4-11	*Benefactor*

The Holy Spirit fills these and many other roles in the believer's life. As you read the Bible, keep your eyes open for other ministries of the Holy Spirit.

After completing this assignment, reflect upon God the Holy Spirit who indwells you as a disciple of Christ. Take a moment in prayer to thank God for the Holy Spirit in your life.

In a group setting, this may be silent or corporate prayer. It may be followed by a discussion of the Holy Spirit's ministry in the Christian's life, or the session may end with the prayer time. You decide what approach would be most comfortable and profitable for your group.

STUDY THREE
The Will of God

Walking into the Scriptures

Read Matthew 12:46-50

1. What question did Jesus ask in this passage?
Who is my mother and who are my brothers?

2. To whom did Jesus point in answering His own question?
His disciples

3. What did Jesus say is the deciding factor in being one of His "relatives"?
His "relatives" are determined by obedience to the Father's will.

Read Mark 14:32-36

1. What was Jesus' mood at this moment in His life?
Deeply distressed and troubled

2. What did Jesus ask of His Father regarding the task which was ahead of Him?
Take the cup of suffering from Me.

3. What was Jesus' final word on the matter?
Not My will, but Your will.

Read Proverbs 3:5-6

1. In whom should we trust and to what extent should we trust?
In the Lord—with all our heart

2. What should we not lean on?
Our own understanding

3. What is the result of acknowledging the Lord?
He will make my path straight.

Read Proverbs 15:22

1. Why do plans fail?
For lack of counsel

2. What factor for success is suggested in this passage?
Many advisors

3. Who might be included in your network of counselors?
*Christian family members   Christian friends
Christian counselors   Pastor
Experts in the area of concern*

Walking It into My Life

Read Exodus 20:1-17

1. Using the Ten Commandments, make a list of ten actions that would be outside the will of God.
    a. *Putting job, hobbies, etc., before God*
    b. *"Worshiping" money, sports stars, politicians, etc.*
    c. *"Swearing"*
    d. *Working on Sunday, working seven days a week*
    e. *Abusing one's parents, the elderly*
    f. *Murder (Consider Matthew 5:21-22.)*

g. *Adultery (Consider Matthew 5:27-30.)*
h. *Stealing*
i. *Lying*
j. *The irrational desire to possess that which belongs to another*

2. Now make a list of three behaviors outside the will of God that commonly occur in today's society. How do these differ from your list from question 1? How are they similar?

Examples of common modern sins which directly relate to the Ten Commandments could include adultery, lying, coveting, stealing and murder. However, some behaviors are so common as to go "unnoticed," such as cheating on expense accounts and tax returns.

If we as a society would faithfully follow what God gave to us 3,500 years ago, virtually all the wrongdoing in our culture would be eliminated. We would be a society operating within God's will.

3. Read First Peter 4:1-6 and First John 2:17. Identify one area where you are or may be headed outside God's will for your life. Pray to God for the power to have victory in this area.

Unless you are convinced that your group has built a significant level of trust, you should avoid making this into a group confession time.

Read Ephesians 6:5-8

1. To be in the will of God, what is to be the Christian's standard of performance at work or school?
We should strive for excellence.

2. What should not be our primary motivation to do well at work or school? What should be our incentive to do well?
We should not try to win the favor of our boss or teacher just to "get ahead." We should do our work as if it were a service to the Lord—and it is, since we are being a witness for Christ.

Walking a Little Deeper

Read Proverbs 15:22

1. List the significant decisions you are facing over the next several months. Search the Word of God and pray about them. Gather the appropriate information that may be needed. In addition, seek the counsel of two or three mature Christians.

If you are doing this study with a group, be prepared to discuss what you thought of while following the steps described above. Do you believe you will be in the will of God?

You may want to consider a discussion on what types of decisions and options could be in the will of God for the individual. Our gracious God does often permit us considerable latitude in making decisions.

2. This discussion of the will of God may bring to mind your will—the legal document that tells what you want done with what you have left behind after you die. Most people seek the counsel of an attorney in doing this. Consider writing your "will" for what you want done with the life you still have—the will of God for your life. Remember as a Christian you have an "attorney" (advocate) with the Father (1 John 2:1, KJV) and a counselor (John 14:26; see also Study Two) to guide and intercede on your behalf (Romans 8:26-27).

Lead a group discussion about this assignment. How did people feel while doing it? What do they think about the result? How do they think this will impact the way they will live for the Lord?

STUDY FOUR
Suffering and Healing

Walking into the Scriptures

Read Romans 5:1-5

1. In Romans 5:1, how does Paul describe the people he is speaking about?
   Justified by faith

2. What are the two things we are to rejoice in?
   a. In the hope of the glory of God
   b. In our sufferings

3. What does suffering produce?
   Perseverance

4. What has God poured into our hearts?
   The Holy Spirit

Read First Peter 2:19-24

1. What kind of suffering is commendable before God?
   Unjust suffering

2. Who suffered for you?
   Christ

3. Where are you to walk?
   "In His steps"

4. What is the remedy for unjust treatment?
   Entrust yourself to Him who judges justly (vs. 23).

Read Second Corinthians 12:7-10

1. How many times did Paul pray for his "thorn in the flesh" to be taken away?
   Three times

2. What did the Lord tell Paul was the alternative to his healing?
   God's grace

3. Rather than boasting about his strengths and gifts, what did Paul tell the Corinthians he boasted about?
   His weaknesses

4. When was Paul strong?
   When he was weak

Read James 5:14-18

1. Whom should the sick person call?
   The elders of the church

2. How should the elders anoint the sick person and in whose name?
   With oil—in the name of the Lord

3. According to James 5:16, what two actions are we to take toward each other?
   a. Confess our sins to one another
   b. Pray for one another

4. What is James' description of Elijah?
   A man just like us

5. What was Elijah able to accomplish?
   He withheld rain, then he prompted rain.

Walking It into My Life

1. Read the scriptural account of the life of Job in chapters 1, 2 and 42 of the book of Job. What adversities did Job encounter (Job 1-2)? How did Job respond and not respond (see 1:21 and 2:10)? Did Job lose all hope in his sufferings (see 13:15)? How did the story of Job's life end (chapter 42)?

Job suffered loss of property, wealth, dignity, family and health. He responded by continuing to praise the Lord; he did not sin against God. Through it all, Job did not lose hope; his hope was steadfast in the Lord. In the end Job was blessed abundantly through his sufferings.

2. List some reasons for suffering based on Scripture.

> *a. John 9:1-3: Suffering is sometimes permitted to give opportunity for testimony of God's power.*
> *b. Romans 8:28-29: Suffering may be good for us; God will work His purpose in our lives through adversity so that we become more Christlike.*
> *c. 2 Corinthians 1:3-4: Suffering can equip us to minister comfort to others in their need.*
> *d. Philippians 1:29: Adversity can be a gift from God to build up one's faith.*
> *e. Hebrews 12:5-11: Corrective action due to sin and disobedience is a possibility.*

If you are doing this study in a group, be prepared to discuss how the Lord has used one of the above reasons for suffering in your life.

As leader be sensitive to the experiences of the group while trying to keep the conversation focused on how the Lord uses suffering in a constructive way in the Christian's life.

Walking a Little Deeper

1. Based on the following Scriptures, let's develop a brief statement concerning divine healing.

> *a. Exodus 15:26: The Lord does the healing.*
> *b. James 5:13-16: As obedient Christians we should ask the elders to anoint us and pray for our healing.*
> *c. James 1:6: We need to believe God can and does still heal.*

    d. Philippians 4:6-7: We should ask for healing with thankful hearts, surrendering our anxiety and experiencing His peace.

    e. 1 Thessalonians 5:17: We should be steadfast in our petitions.

    f. 2 Corinthians 12:7-9: We must recognize that God's purpose is not always the same as ours. His ways are better. He does provide the grace needed to persevere.

Before the next meeting (if you are doing this study in a group), find someone you know who is suffering through an illness. Visit the ill person (perhaps in the company of a mature Christian), share what you have learned and pray for that person's healing. Encourage that person to seek the elders of the church for anointing and prayer.

Encourage the members of the group to share their experiences.

2. Have you ever personally experienced the Lord's divine healing in your life? If not, are you aware of someone else who has? (If you are doing this study in a group, be prepared to share one or two experiences with the rest of the class concerning these healing events.) Does divine healing mean that a person will not get sick again or die?

After a time of sharing, have a brief "praise service" for what God has done.

Experiencing divine healing does not mean a person will not get sick again or die. Even Lazarus, whom Jesus raised from the dead, ultimately died physically.

STUDY FIVE
Missions

Walking into the Scriptures

Read Matthew 28:19-20

1. What does Jesus say His disciples are to do in all nations?
Go and make disciples

2. Baptism is to be done in whose name?
In the name of the Father, Son and Holy Spirit

3. What are we to teach those who respond to the message?
To obey everything Jesus commanded

4. What promise does Jesus give, which will extend to the end of the age?
"I am with you always."

Read Revelation 7:9-11

1. How many were in the great multitude?
No one could count them.

2. Who made up the great multitude?
Persons from every nation, tribe, people and language

3. What was the cry of the great multitude?
"Salvation belongs to our God, who sits on the throne, and to the Lamb."

Read Matthew 9:35-38

1. When Jesus saw the crowds, what "word picture" did He compare them to?
Sheep without a shepherd

2. What was plentiful?
   The harvest

3. What was in short supply?
   The workers

4. What are we to ask the Lord of the harvest to do?
   To send out workers

Walking It into My Life

Read Matthew 24:14

Many today see in this verse of Scripture a motivation for missions. It is sometimes referred to as "bringing back the King." What do you think this phrase means?

The gospel will be preached in the **whole world** *as a testimony to* **all nations or peoples***, and then the end of this age— when Jesus will return—will occur. "Bringing back the King" means that as God's people we have a part in building up the kingdom through the spreading of the gospel message in preparation for the soon return of the King, Jesus Christ.*

Read Acts 1:8

1. What is the necessary prerequisite for successful witnessing and missions?
   We must first receive power from the Holy Spirit.

2. Notice the geography of witnessing, as stated in this verse: first Jerusalem (locally), then Judea (the surrounding region), then Samaria (the region to the north) and finally to the very ends of the earth. What part of the world is not included?
   No part of the world is left out; all is included.

3. List your Jerusalem, Judea, Samaria, etc. Suggest how you might impact each of these areas for the Lord.

For example:

Jerusalem = *my town. Impact through personal witness and prayer.*

Judea = *my extended community, metropolitan area, state or province. Impact through prayer and support of local and regional church ministries.*

Samaria = *my country. Impact through prayer and support of national church and other evangelistic efforts.*

Ends of the earth = *the rest of my world—in other words, foreign missions. Impact through prayer and support of global missionary efforts. Consider personally going to a mission field.*

Walking a Little Deeper

Read Romans 10:12-17

1. For whom is the gospel message intended? Is anyone not to have the opportunity to hear the good news? With whom do you need to share the good news where God has placed you? Pray for the opportunity to be a good witness for Christ.

The gospel is for both Jew and Gentile, that is, all who have yet to believe. The mission is for all to hear the good news, for "Everyone who calls on the name of the Lord will be saved" (Romans 10:13).

Each of us has a number of unsaved people within our sphere of influence. We need to identify them and pray for them, asking the Holy Spirit to provide opportunities for us to share the good news. (If you would like to learn more about how to do this, get the "Walking with the Word" Bible study Webs of Influence by John and Mimi Soper.)

2. List the words of action (verbs) in verses 14 and 15. What is the sequence of events leading to salvation? Who does the preaching of the good news? (Note that the Greek word for "sent" in verse 15 is apostello, which literally means "to send out on a mission," from which we get the words apostle and missionary.)

The action words include call, believe, heard, preaching and sent. For someone to **call** on the name of the Lord and be saved, he must first **believe**. He can only **believe** when he has **heard** the good news. He will **hear** the good news when someone, a missionary, has been **sent** to **preach** the good news. One needs to be **sent** out to **preach** the good news; the one **sent** out is called a missionary.

3. Based on verse 16, will everyone who hears the good news accept it? What does this say concerning successful missions?

Not everyone who hears will call on the name of the Lord and be saved. Success in missions is not based how many believe but how faithful we are in proclaiming the good news to lost people. Many missionaries have labored hard and faithfully with little apparent fruit from their endeavors. This has been true of much of the Muslim world, for example.

4. To get a better understanding of what missions is all about, go to your church library and read the biography of a missionary.

If you are doing this study in a group, be prepared to briefly discuss the missionary's life and mission.

As leader you might suggest one of the books from the Jaffray Collection of Missionary Portraits, published by Christian Publications, Inc. These are lively and easy-to-read accounts of mostly contemporary missions work.

5. There are at least three ways to support missions: You can pray, give and go. Identify a specific mission field and missionary to pray for over the next year. Consider what the Lord would have you joyfully give, from the resources He has given you, to the work of missions. Then do it! Prayerfully consider what your mission field is and whether God is calling you to another field of ministry.

Challenge each person to pray, give and consider whether they are called to go.

STUDY SIX
The Second Coming

Walking into the Scriptures

Read Matthew 24:42-44

1. What are we to do until the day of Jesus' return?
Keep watch and be ready

2. What is unknown even to the believer?
The day of the Lord's return

3. To what does Jesus compare His second coming?
A thief breaking into a house

Read Matthew 25:1-13

1. What is the kingdom of heaven compared to?
Ten virgins on their way to a wedding

2. How are these virgins described in verse 2?
Five were wise, five were foolish.

3. What happened because of the bridegroom's delay?
The virgins became drowsy and fell asleep.

4. Who made it into the banquet?
The wise virgins who had oil

Read Acts 1:7-11

1. What did Jesus say regarding times and dates?
It is not for you to know them.

2. What happened to Jesus in verse 9?
He was taken up.

3. Where were the disciples looking?
Intently into the sky

4. What did the two men dressed in white tell them?
Don't stand here looking up—Jesus will return the same way as He left.

Read Revelation 22:12-14

1. When did Jesus say He was coming?
Soon

2. What will Jesus bring with Him?
My reward

3. What are His titles in verse 13?
   a. Alpha and Omega
   b. First and Last
   c. Beginning and End

4. What two privileges are extended to those whose robes are washed?
   a. The right to the tree of life
   b. May go through the gates into the city

Walking It into My Life

Read Titus 2:11-14

1. Based on Paul's teaching from his letter to Titus, as Christians waiting for the "blessed hope," what things should we not be doing?
   a. Should not be conducting ourselves in an ungodly manner
   b. Should refrain from worldly passions

2. What should Christians be doing?
   a. Live godly, disciplined lives
   b. Be people who can wait
   c. Commit everything in our lives to Christ
   d. Look for ways to do good

3. Identify (if you are in a group study, be prepared to discuss) at least one way this teaching on the second coming should impact your daily life.

Minimally, a clear understanding of the imminent or soon return of Jesus Christ should impact the priorities of our lives. Our goals and plans should become less worldly and "now" centered and more godly and "soon-to-be" focused.

Take time right now to have prayer for the group members concerning their daily lives for Christ.

Read First Thessalonians 4:13-5:11

1. Look up in a dictionary the term "rapture" and write a definition.

The state of being carried away with joy

2. What are the heavenly signs the rapture is occurring, and what is the location of Jesus at the rapture?
   a. The Lord comes down from heaven.
   b. There will a loud command with the voice of the archangel.
   c. The trumpet call of God will sound.
   d. Jesus is in the clouds of the air.

3. What is the sequence of events at the rapture?
   Those believers who have died will rise first, then the believers who are alive at the time of the rapture will rise to the clouds. All believers will live with the Lord forever.

4. In what ways is the truth of this text an encouragement to you? (If you are in a group study, be prepared to discuss this question.)

As Christians we will truly experience the reality of eternal life with the Lord. We will escape the wrath of God's judgment.

Walking a Little Deeper

Read Revelation 20:1-6

1. What terms are used to refer to the devil?
   Dragon, the ancient serpent, the devil and Satan

2. Whom does the beast represent? (See Revelation 13:2b, 4.)
   The Antichrist

3. Who will experience the first resurrection? Who will not?
   Believers will experience the first resurrection. Nonbelievers will not. This a resurrection to life.

4. Who will experience the second death? Who will not?
   Nonbelievers will experience the second death, eternal destruction and torment. Believers will not because they have eternal life. Their names are written in the Lamb's Book of Life.

5. Who will reign with Christ with authority for the thousand years?
   Those who believe in Him—you and I.

In Luke 21:36, Jesus exhorts us to be on the watch and to pray for ourselves concerning the soon coming end-time events. Write down your thoughts on why He might have chosen to emphasize watching and praying.
   To watch is "to look forward to with great expectation." Just because Jesus has not returned in the past 2,000 years we should not lessen our expectancy of His soon return. And, we should pray for ourselves because Jesus has expressed some doubt as to whether He will "find faith on the earth" upon His return (Luke 18:8). The truth of the second coming should motivate Christians to a deeper faith in Christ and a stronger desire to worship and serve Him.

Books by Arnold Fleagle

Developing Your Secret Closet of Prayer
(with Richard Burr)
First Peter
Foundations I (with John Cervone)
Foundations II (with John Cervone)
Journey to Bethlehem
Planted by the Water

A companion Bible study, *Foundations I*,
includes lessons on the following topics:

The Assurance of Salvation
Studying the Scriptures
Prayer
Witnessing
Worship and Fellowship
Stewardship